NATIONAL GEOGRAPHIC

D0503789

We Use Water

Nick Bruce

We use water to drink.

We use water to cook.

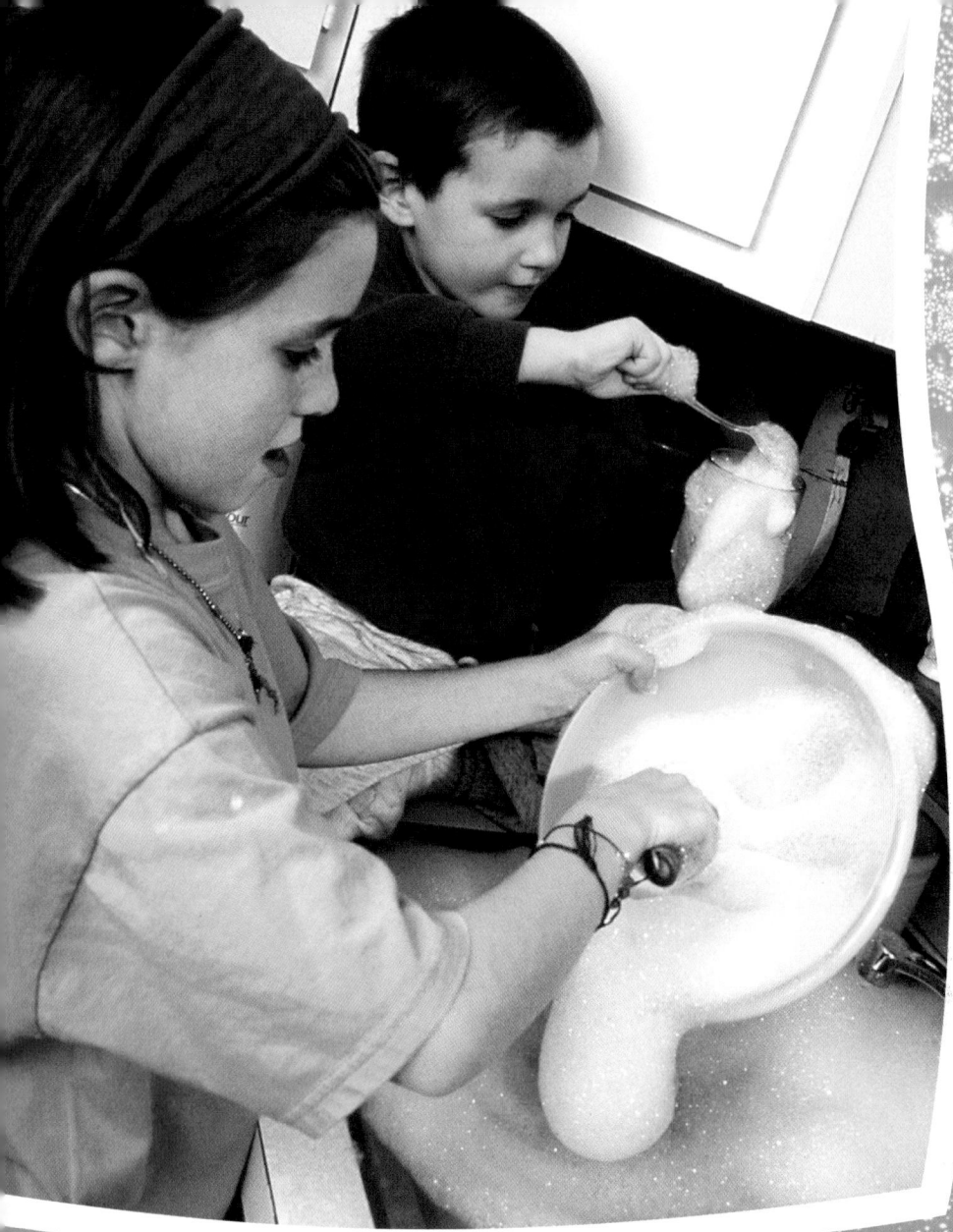

We use water to wash the dishes

We use water to wash our car.

We use water to wash our hands

We use water to grow plants.

We use water to play.